This book is a Gift

from

....

to

....

on the occasion of

....

date

....

I pray that through this book, the Blessing
of His Bleeding will become real in your life;
and that the power of the Blood will be
proven true in your life, in the Precious Name
of Jesus Christ. Amen!

Because of Calvary, you can stand boldly and say, "I OWE THE DEVIL NOTHING!""

POWER IN THE DEATH AND SHED BLOOD OF JESUS CHRIST

The Blessing of His Bleeding

Power in the Death and Shed Blood of Jesus Christ

PAUL ENENCHE MD

For further information, please contact:

DUNAMIS INT'L GOSPEL CENTRE
P.M.B 1677, Garki - Abuja

Or visit our website: www.dunamisgospel.org
Email: pastorenenche@dunamisgospel.org
For information: info@dunamisgospel.org

or call us on these lines: +2348033144509, +234807233270

Designed in Georgia, Europe; Printed in the United States of America by **Kings View Publishing House**
(www.kingsviewbooks.com)

Lord we thank You
for Your kindness
In sending us Your Son
Lord we thank You
for Your mercy
That took Him to the Cross...

We Thank You For Your Love

Song Received and Written
by Dr. (Pst.) Paul Enenche

1. Blessed Jesus, what a gesture it is
to give Your life for the sins of humanity
That was hopelessly lost
A destiny of doom was ours before You came
We stand in awe of You, We magnify You
Lord

CHORUS

Lord we thank You for Your kindness
In sending us Your Son
Lord we thank You for Your mercy
That took Him to the cross
We thank You for Your love
We thank You for Your grace
We thank You for Your Love
We thank You for Your grace

2. Oh! Lord You went to Calvary
To die a gruesome death
You decided to shed Your Blood
To bring us back to God

What Really Happened

from

the CROSS
to the GRAVE
to the RISE?

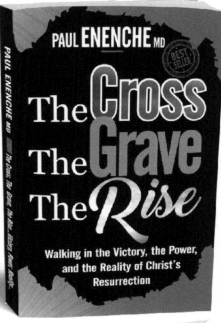

the VICTORY
the POWER
the REALITY
Of Christ's Resurrection

Beloved, next time you are taking the communion, don't just take it because you want to be healthy, or because you want to be delivered from bad dreams. Be target-specific against that unholy appetite; that thing that is not of God. Hold the communion and declare:

"I break your hold by the Blood of Jesus."

CONTENTS

> "At the cross, at the cross
> where I first saw the light
> And the burden of my heart
> rolled away
> It was there by faith
> I received my sight
> And now I am happy all the
> day"

**George S. Schuler
& Isaac Watts**

The **Blessing of His Bleeding** is a revelation of the awesome power inherent in the Cross and Calvary.

Not many people are acquainted with the revelation of the crucifixion, the death, the resurrection, and the power in the Blood of Jesus Christ shed on the Cross of Calvary.

There are, undoubtedly, many 'religious' people who know the story or history behind these events, but they are not connected to the power that can be experienced through them.

That is because the power related to these awesome events is not in *religion* but in *revelation*. You can do many things from the standpoint of religion, but *religion* does not produce reality. It is *revelation* that produces reality.

Deuteronomy 29:29 says, *"The secret things belong unto the Lord our God: but those things which are revealed belong unto us..."*

What is not your revelation can never be your possession. You possess it to the extent it has been revealed.

Beloved, the death of Jesus Christ on the Cross of Calvary is more than just a good Bible story. A solid understanding of the Cross and Calvary can bring an end to the majority of challenges in your life.

I want you to understand that it was at the Cross that Jesus *dismantled* and *de-complicated* the complexities of life. The sacrifice on the Cross was God's solution to our life's complexities.

The peace of God that handles the pressures of life was released at Calvary. And, it is because of what Jesus did on the Cross that we can stand boldly and say, "I owe the devil nothing."

Again, if not for the death of Jesus Christ on the Cross of Calvary, none of us would be righteous enough to approach God.

Without Calvary, we would never have access to the presence of God. But the Cross on which the Son of God died, became the junction where the sons of men could become the sons of God, and gain access to the presence of the Father.

Beyond these, Jesus bled on the Cross, that the blessing of Abraham might come on the Gentiles through Him (Galatians 3:13-14).

So, apart from escaping hell and making heaven - which is the major part of what Jesus came to do - there are other things that His death was meant to handle for us.

What are these things? How can they benefit us? How do we appropriate or make them a reality in our lives? That is what this book aims to help you achieve by His grace.

While reading this book, I implore you to be sensitive to the Holy Spirit and let Him speak to you personally and address any situations, circumstances, or destiny matters in your life.

At some points, you may feel the need to pause and pray, make some declarations, or write down necessary action steps that the Lord impresses on your heart for a change.

If that happens, please follow the leading in your spirit.

It is my prayer, that after reading The Blessing of His Bleeding, you will be able, both to appropriate and to walk in the reality or manifestation of these blessings, in Jesus' Name.

Amen!

The sinless Son of God PAID for the sinful consequences of the sinful acts of sinful men. That is what CALVARY signifies."

Chapter One

THE CROSS AND CALVARY

The
Blessing
of His
Bleeding

"All we like sheep have gone astray; we have turned every one to his own way; and the LORD hath laid on him the iniquity of us all.

Isaiah 53:6

"

1

The Cross and Calvary

> It is because of the Cross that we can boldly say, "I owe the devil NOTHING!"

The revelation of the Cross is of utmost importance in our journey of faith. If we can understand the Cross and Calvary, the majority of challenges we have in life would be over.

The Bible tells us that Jesus was hung on the Cross where He bled, that the Blessing of

Abraham might come on the Gentiles.

Galatians 3:13-14 says,

> *Christ hath redeemed us from the curse of*
> *the law, being made a curse for us: for it is*
> *written, Cursed is every one that hangeth on*
> *a tree: That the blessing of Abraham might*
> *come on the Gentiles through Jesus Christ;*
> *that we might receive the promise of the*
> *Spirit through faith.*

First, we need to understand the Blessing of His bleeding on the Cross. Second, we need to understand our access to that Blessing. These will be unraveled soon.

However, I want to begin by pointing out seven important things regarding the crucifixion or Calvary.

▶▶ **The crucifixion, death, burial, and resurrection of Jesus Christ are the most important, or most powerful things about Christianity.**

To extend it a bit, they are the most important events in the history of mankind.

The birth of the Lord Jesus Christ was very important, but His crucifixion, death, burial, and resurrection were the most important events in the history of mankind.

First, I say that the crucifixion, death, burial, and resurrection of Jesus Christ are the most important and most powerful things about Christianity because, on those occasions, God deployed His Might, Force, Weight, and Energy as the Almighty.

That is what makes 'Christianity' what it is. Colossians 2:13-15 justifies this:

> And you, being dead in your sins and the uncircumcision of your flesh, hath he quickened together with him, having forgiven you all trespasses; Blotting out the handwriting of ordinances that was against us, which was contrary to us, and took it out of the way, nailing it to his cross; And having spoiled principalities and powers, he made a shew of them openly, triumphing over them in it.

The Lord Jesus made a show of principalities openly. That is why His crucifixion, death, burial, and resurrection are the most important events in the history of mankind.

2

» **The best God did for humanity was to give the Best He had to die for the worst in/of men.**

Romans 5:7-8 says, *"For scarcely for a righteous man will one die:..."* (That is, it would be hard for someone to die for a holy person).

> *....yet peradventure for a good man some would even dare to die. But God commendeth his love toward us, in that, while we were yet sinners, Christ died for us.*

The Living Bible makes it even more vivid:

> *Even if we were good, we really wouldn't expect anyone to die for us, though, of course, that might be barely possible. But God showed his great love for us by sending Christ to die for us while we were still sinners* (Romans 5:7-8, TLB).

The Amplified Bible says,

> *Now it is an extraordinary thing for one to give his life even for an upright man, though perhaps for a noble and lovable and generous benefactor someone might even dare to die. But God shows and clearly proves His [own] love for us by the fact that while we were still sinners, (Active sinners) Christ (the Messiah, the Anointed One) died for us.* (Romans 5:7-8, AMP). ✞

Now, look at how rugged the Message Bible puts it:

> *We can understand someone dying for a person worth dying for, and we can understand how someone good and noble could inspire us to selfless sacrifice. But God put his love on the line for us by offering his Son in sacrificial death while we were of no use whatever to him.* (Romans 5:7-8, MSG). ✞

That is what Christianity is all about! God offered His Son in sacrificial death while we were of no use to Him. That is, we were of no benefit to Him.

Besides, there was no hope that we would be anything. There was no hope that we would change. There was no assurance that we would believe in His death.

Even up till now, there are people who do not think God is anything. Yet, God gave His Son to die for us.

So, the best God did for humanity was to give the best He had to die for the worst in (of) men.

The Bible says, *"He spared not his only Son why would He not with him give us all other things"* (Romans 8:32, paraphrased).

》 **The Cross was the place of 'reparation' and 'payment.' And these are the things the Cross symbolizes.**

The sinless Son of God <u>paid</u> for *the sinful consequences of the sinful acts of sinful men.* That is what Calvary signifies.

You probably have heard the song:

 "He paid the debt He did not owe, we owed the debt we could not pay..."

2Corinthians 5:21 says, *"He made him to be sin, who knew no sin; that we might be made the righteousness of God in Christ."* That was what happened! And that is what the Cross signifies.

The sacrifice of Christ on the Cross was God's rescue operation from all claims of the enemy on man.

It is because of the Cross that we can boldly say, "I owe the devil nothing."

1Peter 1:18-19 says, *"Forasmuch as ye know that ye were not <u>redeemed</u> with corruptible things, as silver and gold, from your vain conversation received by tradition from your fathers; But with the precious blood of Christ...."*

The word 'Redeemed' means *rescued, bought back by the Blood of Jesus Christ*. On Calvary, many years ago, Jesus offered Himself to buy us back. 1Corinthians 6:19-20 says, *"you are not your own? For you were bought at a price;"* (NKJV).

The Little Boat

Every time I teach on the price the Lord Jesus paid for our salvation, I remember the story of the *little boat*.

The little boat belonged to a fisherman who took his time to create and carve it very well to his liking.

One day, while the boat was anchored on the seashore, the wind, storm, or whatever it was, cut the anchor, and the little boat floated on top of the sea until it was lost.

Some other fisherman saw the little boat somewhere, harvested it, and sold it. Then someone bought it and put it in his shop on display for sale.

The owner of the little boat looked for it but couldn't find it. It is not that he could not make another boat but he had an attachment to the little boat that he took his time to carve or create.

Suddenly, he heard that a boat that looked like his little boat was on display in a shop.

When he got to the shop, he saw his little boat, recognized it, and told the boat seller that he was the owner of the boat; and that the boat got lost. But the seller could not understand.

The seller said to him, "I'm sorry! I know it is possible that it is your boat and your story sounds true. But I bought the boat. It was sold to me by someone else. All I need is for you to pay me the exact amount I paid to get the boat, and you will get it back."

Obviously, the man agreed with the boat seller not to sell the boat to anyone else, that he was coming to buy it.

He had to go and labour until he was able to raise the required amount. Then he returned to the seller and bought the boat.

He carried the boat with so much excitement and celebration. Then he sat down, tapping the boat as if it were a person.

Looking at the little boat he said,

"Little boat! Little boat! I now own you twice. First, I created you and now, I have bought you. I am your owner twice.

"I created you, manufactured you with my hands. You got lost. Then I went and paid for you again. Even though I owned you; even though I made you; because you got lost and got sold off, I had to pay again to buy you; so I am now your owner twice."

That is how every born again child of God is. God is our owner twice. He made us, created us in His Image and we got lost - hopelessly lost in sin, traditions, and the things of this life. And He sent His Son Jesus to die for us and buy us back.

 So, WE ARE HIS 'CREATURE' AND WE ARE HIS 'PROPERTY.' HE CREATED US, THEN HE REDEEMED US. HE IS OUR OWNER TWICE.

That is what Calvary is all about.

The Cross is the place of payment, the place of reparation, and the place of rescue.

The sacrifice of Christ on the Cross of Calvary was God's solution to the complexities of man's challenges. The Cross was and is our solution spot.

Beloved, every time you are surrounded with complexities of situations, remember the Cross.

In Matthew 1:21, concerning Jesus, the Bible said, "*And she shall bring forth a son, and thou shalt call his name JESUS: for he shall save his people from their sins.*"

'Save' means 'solve' - He shall solve the sin problem of His people. He shall dismantle and de-complicate the complexities of the people.

THERE IS NO PROBLEM OR CHALLENGE YOU HAVE AS A PERSON THAT IS NOT 'HANDLEABLE' BY THE CROSS (Matthew 1:21).

The sacrifice on the Cross was God's solution to man's complexities.

6

The sacrifice of Christ on the Cross was the facilitator of the reunion of God and man.

2Corinthians 5:17-18 says, *"Therefore if any man be in Christ, he is a new creature: old things are passed away; behold, all things are become new. And all things are of God, who hath reconciled us to himself by Jesus Christ, and hath given to us the ministry of reconciliation;"*

THE CROSS IS THE JUNCTION OF RECONCILIATION; IT IS THE JUNCTION OF REUNION. IT IS THE JUNCTION OF RECONNECTION BETWEEN GOD AND MAN.

Man was hopelessly lost after God drove Adam from the Garden of Eden. People began to wander into 'all manner' of religion in search of God.

Now, that is the difference between Christianity and religion. Religion is man searching for God while Christianity is God searching for man. God searched for man by sending His Son, Jesus to locate man. That is why we are children of God today.

>> **The Cross of Calvary was and is the junction of exchange of man's worst for God's best.**

The sacrifice on the Cross facilitated what I call *The Great Exchange*. The worst of man was exchanged for the Best of God at the Cross of Calvary.

The Cross became the *Humano-Divinity Junction*: a junction where the Son of God became the Son of man and made it possible for the sons of men to become the sons of God; a crossover junction where people bound for hell can change direction.

Oh, the love that drew salvation's plan!
Oh, the grace that brought it down to man!
Oh, the mighty gulf that God did span,
At Calvary.

"Mercy there was great, and grace was free;
Pardon there was multiplied to me;
There my burdened soul found liberty,
At Calvary."

William R. Newell

31

But that's not all!

Beloved, Jesus did not only die so that you can escape hell and go to heaven. That is the major part of it; in fact, the most important. But there are other things that His death was meant to handle for you.

What are these other things?

That is what we will see in the next chapter as we turn our focus on *the exchange of the Cross*.

The Son of God became the Son of man and made it possible for the sons of men to become the sons of God.

Chapter Two

THE GREAT EXCHANGE - 1

The
Blessing
of His
Bleeding

"For he hath made him to be sin for us, who knew no sin; that we might be made the righteousness of God in him.

2 Corinthians 5:21

,,

2

The Great Exchange -1

" The welfare of man is in the package of Redemption. Living pitiable and beggarly is not your portion."

To understand the Blessing of His Bleeding, we must understand the 'Great Exchange' that took place when Jesus died on the Cross of Calvary.

So, what was the exchange?

» **Jesus took our unrighteousness so that we can take on His righteousness.**

2Corinthians 5:21 says, *"For he hath made him to be sin for us, who knew no sin; <u>that we might be made the righteousness of God in him</u>."*

Jesus took our unrighteousness, filthiness, and sinfulness, so that we can take on His righteousness.

 IF NOT FOR THE DEATH OF CHRIST ON CALVARY, NONE OF US WOULD BE RIGHTEOUS ENOUGH TO APPROACH GOD.

It is by the righteousness of God that we walk with God. And by His righteousness we access heaven.

What a faithful God!

Psalms 130:3 says, *"If thou, Lord, shouldest mark iniquities, O Lord, who shall stand?"*

Think about it: Maybe you did not commit fornication or adultery; you did not steal, lie, cheat, or do any of those things. Yet, there may be that tiny pride in your heart that could take you to hell.

There may be that tiny bitterness, jealousy, anger, or whatever it is that you ignore, which the devil might hold against you.

It is the righteousness of Jesus that makes you qualified to be pardoned of such.

He took our unrighteousness so that we can take on His righteousness.

» He took our hurt or pain so we could take His health.

Isaiah 53:5-6 says, *"But he was wounded for our transgressions, he was bruised for our iniquities: the chastisement of our peace was upon him; and with his stripes we are healed. All we like sheep have gone astray; we have turned every one to his own way; and the LORD hath laid on him the iniquity of us all."*

He was hurt that you might be healed. His pain became your gain. The sickness that should have 'sickened' you, 'sickened' Him.

Every affliction or diseases the devil wants you to carry in your lifetime, He already carried them.

> *Therefore, I curse every demon of diseases and affliction tying you down. I declare that diabetes, hypertension, inherited diseases, etc., all come to an end in your life, in the Name of Jesus!*

Beloved, you can claim your healing RIGHT NOW by the power of His death or crucifixion. You can lay hold on the horns of the altar and say,

> *Lord, if this is one reason why You were crucified, then I cannot cross from today into tomorrow with this affliction: this ear condition, eye condition, liver condition, coronavirus symptoms. I cannot cross from today into tomorrow with this affliction."*

"Jesus, keep me near the cross,
There a precious fountain—
Free to all, a healing stream—
Flows from Calv'ry's mountain."

Frances J. Crosby

✛ Take a minute right now and pray in the Holy Ghost concerning any health challenge you are experiencing.

✛ Make demands on the power of His death and that Great Exchange that took place at His crucifixion.

>> **He took our wretchedness so we can take His blessedness. His bleeding was our blessing. His nakedness was our 'clothedness.'**

▸ He had no shelter for His Head.

▸ At Calvary, they stripped Him naked.

▸ He had nothing to drink when He was thirsty. When He asked for water, He was given vinegar.

2Corinthians 8:9 says, "*For ye know the grace of our Lord Jesus Christ, that, though he was rich, yet for your sakes he became poor, that ye through his poverty might be rich.*"

This is Scripture!

He was made poor that we might be rich. He was stripped naked that we might be clothed.

Revelation 5:12 says, *"Worthy is the Lamb that was slain to receive power, and riches, and wisdom, and strength, and honour, and glory, and blessing."*

Part of the reason He was slain was to receive *'riches'* and *'blessing'* on your behalf. So, you are not permitted to carry any generational wretchedness. You are not permitted to transmit generational poverty.

THE WELFARE OF MAN IS IN THE PACKAGE OF REDEMPTION. LIVING PITIABLE AND BEGGARLY IS NOT YOUR PORTION. LIVING AS A SHAME AND REPROACH TO REDEMPTION IS NOT YOUR PORTION.

Christianity is not synonymous with poverty. The Scriptures confirm that He took our wretchedness so we can take His blessedness.

"He was made poor that you might be rich. He was stripped naked that you might be clothed.
"

» He took our 'cursefulness' so we can receive His 'curselessness.'

He took our 'cursefulness' - especially in Africa where there are plenty of curses:

» Inability to get married on time;

» Inability to have children after marriage, etc.

There are 'all manner' of ancestral, generational, family curses, witchcraft manipulation, etc.

Jesus took them all on Calvary.

Galatians 3:13 says, "*Christ hath redeemed us from the curse of the law, being made a curse for us: for it is written, Cursed is every one that hangeth on a tree:*"

He was hanged on a tree that we may receive the blessing of Abraham.

Beloved, it does not matter the family or the village you come from. It does not matter the transactions your father and forefathers entered into.

IT DOES NOT MATTER WHAT BLOOD SACRIFICES HAVE BEEN MADE ON YOUR BEHALF OR THAT OF YOUR LINEAGE. THEY HOLD NO WATER AS FAR AS CALVARY IS CONCERNED.

Jesus could not be cursed. He was 'curseless.' So, you cannot be 'curseful.'

You can make demands on your exemption from the liabilities of your lineage, the calamities of your father's house, and the things that the devil is insisting on imposing on your life.

Today is your day of freedom!

Now Declare!

✝ *Heavenly Father, I declare that Jesus took my cursefulness so I can receive His curselessness.*

✝ *I make demands on my exemption from the liabilities of my lineage, the calamities of my father's house, and the evil manifestations that the devil insists on imposing on my life.*

✝ *I declare my freedom by the power of the Cross of Calvary in the Name of Jesus Christ. Amen!*

> **He took our place in death so we can take His place in life. He died our death so we can live His life - the life He should have lived.**

In John 18:4-6, when the soldiers went to arrest Jesus, He asked them, "Whom seek ye?" they said, "Jesus of Nazareth."

As soon as He said, "I am he," they went backward, and fell to the ground.

John 18:7-8 says, *"Then asked he them again, Whom seek ye? And they said, Jesus of Nazareth. Jesus answered, I have told you that I am he: if therefore ye seek me, let these go their way:"*

That is to say, "the only condition I would surrender Myself to be arrested is that none of My followers would be arrested to die with Me."

John 18:9 says, *"That the saying might be fulfilled, which he spake, Of them which thou gavest me have I lost none."*

Do you understand that?

HE SURRENDERED HIMSELF TO DIE YOUNG SO YOU CAN LIVE LONG. THEREFORE, YOU CAN'T JUST BOW CHEAPLY TO ANY DEMONIC FORCE OF DEATH.

Hebrews 2:9 says, *"But we see Jesus, who was made a little lower than the angels for the suffering of death* (That is, He temporarily accepted to be a man because of death), *crowned with glory and honour; that he by the grace of God should taste death for every man."* (Paraphrased).

That is, He should die your death so you can live His life. He should die young so you can live long.

- Beloved, it does not matter who died prematurely in your lineage.

- It does not matter how surrounded you are with the forces of death.

- It does not matter how many times death has made attempts at you.

Listen! By virtue of Calvary, you are not permitted to die before your time. And you can make that decision and force it to happen today, in the Name of Jesus Christ.

No power of hell, no scheme of man,
Can ever pluck me from His hand:
Till He returns or calls me home,
Here in the power of Christ I'll stand.

Stuart Townend

Christianity is not synonymous with poverty. The Scriptures confirm that He took our wretchedness, so we can take His blessedness.

Chapter Three

THE GREAT EXCHANGE - 2

The *Blessing* of His **Bleeding**

"He is despised and rejected of men; a man of sorrows, and acquainted with grief: and we hid as it were our faces from him; he was despised, and we esteemed him not. But he was wounded for our transgressions, he was bruised for our iniquities: <u>the chastisement of our peace was upon him;</u>

Isaiah 53:3-5

"

3

The Great Exchange -2

"Christ in you is the allocation of DIGNITY.
Christ in you is the allocation of QUALITY."

I believe that an understanding of the Great Exchange on the Cross has helped you to appreciate the Blessing of His Bleeding.

In this chapter, we look further into the "exchange" that took place at the Cross when Jesus died for us.

>> **He was despised so we can be esteemed. He was devalued so we can have value.**

This is very important!

Christianity is an enemy of inferiority - inferiority complex. Isaiah 53:3 says, *"He is despised and rejected of men..."*

That was part of what He had to go through – *despised, rejected, and devalued,* so that you can be 'envalued.'

They negotiated and sold Him for thirty pieces of silver - *the price of a slave -* so that no one can transact on your head and devalue or reduce you to nothing.

Beloved, if you are a real child of God, you are one of those who refuse to die of low self-esteem.

According to John G. Lake, *a child of God is the wildest kind of the most enthusiastic optimists in the world.*

That is, a true child of God is enthusiastic, optimistic, and positivistic.

In fact, as a child of God, you are a bundle of energy - the energy of the One Who values you.

1Peter 2:9 says, "*But ye are a chosen generation, a royal priesthood, an holy nation, a peculiar people...,*"

That is, you are a quality person, not a riff-raff, not a hoodlum, not a despicable entity, not someone to be tolerated or taken for granted.

Many Christians don't know who they are. They don't know what Christ has done for them.

Colossians 1:27-28 says, "*Christ in you the hope of glory*"

 THAT IS, CHRIST IN YOU IS THE ALLOCATION OF DIGNITY. CHRIST IN YOU IS THE ALLOCATION OF QUALITY. CHRIST IN YOU IS THE ENHANCEMENT OF VALUE.

That is why some of us move with a lot of audacity.

I have never felt inferior to anyone anywhere in this world because I am too aware of who I am in Christ.

I believe that what you are reading right now is blasting off every demon of low self-worth and inferiority out of your life.

I do not care how your growing up days were. Perhaps people talked down on you and looked down on you.

Maybe you were never good enough or nothing you did was ever good enough.

Maybe even your mother, father, and siblings don't think you are anything. They have compared you with other people and made you feel worthless.

But Christ in you is the allocation of dignity. Christ in you is the allocation of quality. Christ in you is the enhancement of value.

It does not matter what anyone thinks about you.

Don't forget that David's family never thought he was anything, yet David became somebody.

Beloved, Jesus was despised so you can be esteemed.

He was devalued so you can have value in life.

❱❱ He was rejected so you can be accepted.

One of the greatest challenges in our world today is the challenge of rejection. But Jesus was rejected so you can be accepted.

Put another way, He suffered rejection so you can experience celebration and acceptance.

Isaiah 53:3 tells us *He was despised and rejected of men.*

Can you imagine that the King of kings, the Lord of lords, the I AM THAT I AM, the Rose of Sharon, the One Who was not created, elected, nominated, selected, or appointed by man, was rejected?

So, don't feel too bad that human beings are trying to show rejection on your person in one way or the other. You are not and cannot be rejected. Jesus was rejected so you can be accepted.

Ephesians 1:5-6 says, "*Having predestinated us unto the adoption of children by Jesus Christ to himself, according to the good pleasure of his will, To the praise of the glory of his grace, wherein he hath made us accepted in the beloved."*

So, Jesus made us accepted.

Beloved, you are too accepted by God to be rejected by man. Refuse to allow any demon of rejection to follow you.

✓ Please note this:

It doesn't matter what the circumstances of your birth were. Maybe when your mother gave birth to you, your father denied that he was responsible for the child. And you grew up with rejection.

Or, maybe your case is that of your father abandoning you and your siblings to your mother. And you grew up feeling abandoned and rejected.

Whatever it is that makes you feel abandoned or rejected, I want you to know that Jesus got you covered!

Maybe you were qualified for a position, but you were rejected and it was given to someone else on the grounds of partiality, favouritism, tribalism, nepotism, ethnicity, and clannishness.

God got you covered!

Maybe you were doing so outstandingly well in your workplace, yet they say they don't want you again, and you feel rejected.

 Now hear this:

"If you are a child of God truly doing your best; that is, you are superb and excellent in what you do, that place is not for you. They don't know your value. You are too valuable for them. **99**

Be patient. The real place of your value is coming. In fact, in such a case, you did not lose the job; the job lost you. And in time to come, they will know who you are.

Maybe yours isn't about your job, but rather that a young man says he is not going to marry you anymore, or a young lady says she is not going to marry you again. And maybe, you have experienced that several times.

The truth is that the devil knows your

potential. He is merely trying to rub rejection on you, and it is never your portion.

 Every child of God must know this:

If you are not going to marry someone, please don't give them high hopes. Don't be an agent of rejection like Satan the devil. If you don't want to marry a young lady or a young man, don't lift their hopes."

Real people give value to others. Real children of God - real valuable people - allocate value to others. They are not agents of rejection.

If you are reading this and you are feeling low, inferior, or rejected for any reason, I curse that demon of rejection that makes you feel lower than others. I command it to get out today, in the Name of Jesus. Amen!

Beloved, if you have suffered any form of rejection, you don't need to kill yourself for it.

Maybe a man walked out of your life and left you and your young child, just leave him alone. Let God deal with him. You don't need to die because of another person's behaviour.

CELEBRATE YOURSELF. DECORATE YOURSELF. SHOW THE DEVIL THAT YOU ARE TOO ACCEPTED BY GOD TO BE REJECTED BY MAN.

And, understand that it does not matter what men say, provided, God has said, "Yes" to you.

He took our grief and sorrow so we can take His joy and pleasure.

Do you know that Jesus never knew depression in His entire life on earth? He only cried once at the tomb of Lazarus, and that was for the calamity of humanity. But He became a man of sorrow on the Cross.

Isaiah 53:4 says, "*Surely he hath borne our griefs, and carried our sorrows: yet we did esteem him stricken, smitten of God, and afflicted.*"

He carried our griefs and sorrows on the Cross. The Messianic prophetic writing of Isaiah 61:1-3 was talking about Jesus and what

He was coming to do:

> *The Spirit of the Lord GOD is upon me; because the LORD hath anointed me to preach good tidings unto the meek; he hath sent me to bind up the brokenhearted, to proclaim liberty to the captives, and the opening of the prison to them that are bound; To proclaim the acceptable year of the LORD, and the day of vengeance of our God; <u>to comfort all that mourn; To appoint unto them that mourn in Zion, to give unto them beauty for ashes, the oil of joy for mourning, the garment of praise for the spirit of heaviness...</u>*

In other words, part of His assignment to humanity is to replace your sorrow and grief with joy and pleasure.

That is, you can deploy the Blood of Jesus against every root of consistent grief.

"Whatever it is that makes you feel abandoned or rejected, know that Jesus got you covered.

"

I'll like you to take a minute and make these declarations:

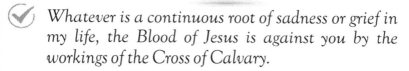

Now Declare!

☑ *Whatever is a continuous root of sadness or grief in my life, the Blood of Jesus is against you by the workings of the Cross of Calvary.*

☑ *Jesus carried my sorrow and grief. Devil, you cannot continue to make me grieve. You cannot continue to cause me pain. You cannot continue to cause me sorrow. I reject you in the Name of Jesus!*

☑ *I curse every root of sorrow by the Blood of Jesus and by the power of the Cross of Calvary, in Jesus' Mighty Name! Amen!*

Maybe you are reading this and you are always experiencing pain, sorrow, grief, and sadness all year round.

Maybe now and then, a negative thing happens around you. The devil has created a chain of events to cause you continuous pain, sorrow, and sadness.

▶ ***Today, by the speakings of the Blood of Jesus, that cycle of sorrow is cut off. It expires now!***

> *That cycle of grief is arrested NOW by the power of the Blood of Jesus, in the Name of Jesus Christ!*

He took your grief and sorrow so you can take His joy and pleasure.

» He took our pressure so we can take His peace.

He took our pressure, trouble, and crisis so we can take His peace.

Isaiah 53:3-5 says, *"He is despised and rejected of men; a man of sorrows, and acquainted with grief: and we hid as it were our faces from him; he was despised, and we esteemed him not. Surely he hath borne our griefs, and carried our sorrows: yet we did esteem him stricken, smitten of God, and afflicted. But he was wounded for our transgressions, he was bruised for our iniquities: the chastisement of our peace was upon him..."*

Anything that was meant to take peace from us was laid on Him. He carried whatever would put our peace under pressure.

The Living Bible says, "*But he was wounded and bruised for our sins. He was beaten that we might have peace; he was lashed-and we were healed!*" (Isaiah 53:3-5).

Did you see that? He was beaten that WE might have peace.

The Amplified Bible says, "*But He was wounded for our transgressions, He was crushed for our wickedness [our sin, our injustice, our wrongdoing]; The punishment [required] for our* **well-being** *fell on Him, And by His stripes (wounds) we are healed*" (Isaiah 53:3-5).

The word "well-being" means "peace." Whatever is needed for us to have peace was laid on Him.

You know, some people are permanently under pressure, living a 'tensed up' life. But Jesus took our pressure, so we can have His peace.

THERE IS A QUALITY OF PEACE FROM THE CROSS, AN ABUNDANCE OF SUPERNATURAL RESOURCES THAT CAN KEEP YOU UNRUFFLED.

In the course of the construction of our Church Worship Auditorium, the Glory Dome, a couple of people who came in contact with me were surprised that I was just at peace.

One front-line Evangelist said to me, "You are so calm; so normal. I was expecting you to be under pressure."

Then he asked me, "Do you sleep at night?"

I said, "I sleep very well."

There was not a trace of worry for one day concerning the season of that construction - not then, not now!

I have seen people come into my office and say, "Oh! the peace around you is so heavy. I don't feel like going."

At one time, my daughter Deborah sat with me in the office, and she said, "Ahh! The whole place is just so peaceful. Everything is so calm; no worry at all."

The peace of God is an asset.

Beloved, the devil aims to put you

permanently under pressure. He wants to make you worry over one thing after another permanently. But Calvary guarantees your peace. That is why Jesus is called The Prince of Peace.

 From today, by the power of Calvary, I declare the expiration of every form of pressure and trouble in your life, in the Name of Jesus.

10

» He took your place in hell so you can find your place in heaven.

Now, you may ask, "How is that?"

Well, between the crucifixion and the resurrection, part of the pathway included a passage through hell. That was where Jesus spoilt principalities and powers and made a show of them openly.

He went to the headquarters of demons and defeated them.

You know, Jesus could not have said, "All power in heaven and on earth is given unto

Me," if He did not go to Satan's headquarters and defeat him there.

The Messianic Psalmist, David, spoke about it:

> *I have set the LORD always before me: because he is at my right hand, I shall not be moved. Therefore my heart is glad, and my glory rejoiceth: my flesh also shall rest in hope. For thou wilt not leave my soul in hell; neither wilt thou suffer thine Holy One to see corruption. Thou wilt shew me the path of life (That is what led to resurrection): in thy presence is fulness of joy; at thy right hand there are pleasures for evermore.* **Psalms 16:8-11**, emphasis mine.

The claims of justice had to be met. Romans 3:23 says, "*All have sinned and fallen short of the glory of God.*" And Romans 6:23 says, "*The wages of sin is death.*" That death is eternal hell.

Now, if Jesus was to take our sins and bear our consequences, He was meant to pass through whatever we were meant to pass through.

He suffered for all of humanity all at once within three days.

You can imagine the eternities of suffering laid on Him.

The Apostle Peter made it clearer in Acts 2:22-28 when he said,

> *Ye men of Israel, hear these words; Jesus of Nazareth, a man approved of God among you by miracles and wonders and signs, which God did by him in the midst of you, as ye yourselves also know: Him, being delivered by the determinate counsel and foreknowledge of God, ye have taken, and by wicked hands have crucified and slain: Whom God hath raised up, having loosed the pains of death: because it was not possible that he should be holden of it. For David speaketh concerning him, I foresaw the Lord always before my face, for he is on my right hand, that I should not be moved: Therefore did my heart rejoice, and my tongue was glad; moreover also my flesh shall rest in hope: Because thou wilt not leave my soul in hell, neither wilt thou suffer thine Holy One to see corruption. Thou hast made known to me the ways of life; thou shalt make me full of joy with thy countenance.* ✝

Do you know the meaning of that?

It means, for anyone who ends in hell, it is their choice. Jesus already passed through that way so you don't end there.

There was One Who was willing to die in my stead,
That a soul so unworthy might live;
And the path to the cross He was willing to tread,
All the sins of my life to forgive.

"They are nailed to the cross!
They are nailed to the cross!
Oh, how much He was willing to bear!
With what anguish and loss Jesus went to the cross,
But He carried my sins with Him there."

Carrie E. Breck

Celebrate yourself. Decorate yourself. Show the devil that you are too accepted by God to be rejected by man.

"What can we do without the Blood? What is Christianity without the Blood? What is Christian victory without the Blood?"

Chapter Four

THE POWER OF THE BLOOD

The Blessing of His Bleeding

"Forasmuch as ye know that ye were not redeemed with corruptible things, as silver and gold, from your vain conversation received by tradition from your fathers; But with the precious blood of Christ, as of a lamb without blemish and without spot:"

1 Peter 1:18-19

The Power of the Blood

" Satan! THE BLOOD OF JESUS is
against you!"

Most of the greatest Blessings we could ever gain from the Bleeding of our Lord are found in the Precious Blood He shed on the Cross of Calvary.

Some people say Christianity talks about

blood all the time. Oh yes! That's because the foundation of Christianity was laid in the Blood of the Founder. There can be no Christianity without Blood - the Precious Blood of Jesus Christ.

1Peter 1:18-19 (NLT) says, *"For you know that God paid a ransom to save you from the empty life you inherited from your ancestors. And the ransom he paid was not mere gold or silver. It was the precious blood of Christ, the sinless, spotless Lamb of God."*

In this chapter, we are looking at the Blessings in the Blood that oozed from His bleeding side. We are looking at the power in that Precious Blood.

So, what are the blessings, the benefits, or the power of the Precious Blood of Jesus Christ?

» The Blood is our weapon of exemption from enemy plagues and destruction.

The reason why any plague ravaging the world is not permitted to affect you, is the Blood.

Exodus 12:12-13 says, *"For I will pass through the land of Egypt this night, and will smite all the firstborn in the land of Egypt, both man and beast; and against all the gods of Egypt I will execute judgment: I am the LORD. And the blood shall be to you for a token upon the houses where ye are: and when I see the blood, I will pass over you, and the plague shall not be upon you to destroy you, when I smite the land of Egypt."*

The Bible says, "When I see the blood, I will pass over you..." Anything that sees the Blood must pass over you. That includes *Coronavirus, Ebola virus, Lassa fever, calamities, disasters, and premature death.*

The Blood is your weapon of exemption from any kind of enemy plague and destruction.

» **The Blood is our weapon of escape from enemy captivity and imprisonment.**

You come out of enemy prison houses by the weapon of the Blood.

71

Zechariah 9:11-12 says, "As for thee also, by the blood of thy covenant I have sent forth thy prisoners out of the pit wherein is no water. Turn you to the strong hold, ye prisoners of hope: even to day do I declare that I will render double unto thee;"

This Scripture says, "Turn you to the stronghold." That Stronghold is 'The Blood.'

It says, by the Blood of the covenant, the prisoners are sent out of the pit.

The New International Version makes this clearer:

"As for you, because of the blood of my covenant with you, I will free your prisoners from the waterless pit" (Zechariah 9:11).

Because of the Blood of the covenant, you can escape the enemy's captivity and imprisonment.

ANY PRISON THE ENEMY KEPT YOU - THE PRISON OF ADDICTION, CAPTIVITY OF LIMITATION, OR WHATEVER IMPRISONMENT YOU FIND YOURSELF, YOU CAN BREAK FREE BY THE POWER OF THE BLOOD.

You can say,

> *Lord why I'm I here? What has kept my life in this kind of prison? I break free from this limitation by the Blood of Jesus Christ!*

The Blood is our escape from the enemy's prison.

3

The Blood is our tonic of Divine health and Divine life.

Connection to the Life of God happens by the Blood.

The Blood of Jesus is our tonic of Divine Health and Divine life.

In John 6:54-57, Jesus said, "*Whoso eateth my flesh, and drinketh my blood, hath eternal life; and I will raise him up at the last day. For my flesh is meat indeed, and my blood is drink indeed. He that eateth my flesh, and drinketh my blood, dwelleth in me, and I in him. As the living Father hath sent me, and I live by the Father: so he that eateth me, even he shall live by me.*"

What that means is, you connect life and health from His Blood. For the life of all flesh is in the blood, according to Leviticus 17:11.

So, connecting the Blood of Jesus is connecting His life - His sickless, vibrant, quality, abundant life.

The Blood is your tonic for Divine health and Divine life.

» **The Blood is our channel of blessing. It is our connector with the blessing of God.**

In 1Corinthians 10:16, Paul the Apostle speaking about the communion cup said,

The cup of blessing which we bless, is it not the communion of the blood of Christ?...

The communion cup is called the cup of the blessing. As we partake of the communion, the Blood becomes our channel of blessing; it is our connector to the blessing of God.

What is the meaning of that?

It means that the way light cannot co-exist with darkness, the blessing cannot co-exist with curses.

Again, the way life and death cannot exist together, the blessing cannot co-exist with curses.

 IF THE BLOOD CONNECTS YOU WITH THE BLESSING, IT MEANS IT DISCONNECTS YOU FROM CURSES.

This is why the Bible says, *"Christ has redeemed us from the curse of the law, being made a curse for us, for it is written curse is everyone that hangeth on a tree that the blessing of Abraham might come upon the Gentiles"* (Galatians 3:13-14).

The meaning of that is, as you are connected to the Blood, the blessing gets connected to you and the curses of your life - *ancestral, generational, witchcraft, or occultic*, get disconnected from your life.

The enemy's ancestral and witchcraft curses cannot function in your life when you are connected to the Blood.

What a treasure it is to be connected to the Blood. One of the songs we sing often says,

By your Blood O' Lord.
By your Blood O' Lord.
By your Blood O' Lord you set the captive free...

So, get set! If there is any curse working against you, by the Blood of Jesus that curse is broken forever!

The Blood is our weapon of victory in battle over the enemy.

The Blood is our weapon of victory in battle; for we overcome the devil by the Blood of the Lamb and by the word of our testimony (Revelations 12:11).

When you are surrounded by battles you don't understand, declare:

Satan the Blood of Jesus is against you!

Plead the Blood of Jesus against the enemy's

conspiracy against you in your office, community, or family.

Plead the Blood of Jesus against sudden demonic conspiracy against your children, husband, or wife.

If you realize that suddenly they are behaving in ways you don't understand, declare:

- *Satan the Blood of Jesus is against you regarding this child or this man.*

- *The Blood of Jesus is against you concerning the issue of my work.*

- *The Blood of Jesus is against you concerning my health.*

- *The Blood of Jesus is against you in our nation.*

- *The Blood of Jesus is against you in my finances. I have done everything I am meant to do: I am a giver; I am a tither. You have no place in my finances. The Blood of Jesus is against you.*

- *I overcome you by the Blood of Jesus.*

- *I bring you into defeat by the Blood of Jesus. I obtain victory over you by the tokens of the Blood.*

Beloved, what can we do without the Blood? What is Christianity without the Blood? What is Christian victory without the Blood? It is our weapon of victory in battle over the enemy.

6

» The Blood is our instrument of cleansing and purification.

Hebrews 9:13-14 says, *"For if the blood of bulls and of goats, and the ashes of an heifer sprinkling the unclean, sanctifieth to the purifying of the flesh: How much more shall the blood of Christ, who through the eternal Spirit offered himself without spot to God, purge your conscience from dead works to serve the living God?"*

The Blood of Jesus Christ purges our conscience from dead works to serve the Living God.

1John 1:7 says, *"But if we walk in the light, as he is in the light, we have fellowship one with another, and the blood of Jesus Christ his Son cleanseth us from all sin."*

The Blood purges us from sin.

The Blood is the reason why the spirit of masturbation, lesbianism, homosexuality, gambling, lying, cheating, bitterness, unforgiveness, pride, arrogance, haughtiness, anger, or uncontrolled temper, cannot continue to hold your life to ransom.

The Blood of Jesus is the reason why you cannot live such a low life of picking things that are not yours. The Blood breaks the hold of iniquity off your life.

Now, the Blood of Jesus is not just what you plead when you have messed up. No! The Blood of Jesus is what gives you victory over that hold of the enemy, that thirst for evil that would not let you rest. The Blood breaks its hold over your life.

I declare by the speakings of the Blood of Jesus, that grip, that hold of iniquity, that hold of sin, that thing that has made you a slave of bad habit is broken right now by the Blood of Jesus, in the Name of Jesus. Amen!

Beloved, next time you are taking the communion, don't just take it because you want to be healthy, or because you want to be delivered from bad dreams. Be target-specific against that unholy appetite; that thing that is not of God.

Hold the communion and declare:

I break your hold by the Blood of Jesus.

The Blood is our instrument of cleansing. It is our instrument of purification. That is one of the blessings of His bleeding.

» **The Blood is our key of access to God's presence.**

A familiar song by Brian Robert Doerksen says, "*I enter the Holy of Holies. I enter through the Blood of the Lamb.*"

You see that?

We enter the Holy of Holies through the Blood of the Lamb.

Hebrews 10:19 says, "*Having therefore, brethren, boldness to enter into the holiest by the blood of Jesus,...*"

So, we access the Holy of Holies by the Blood of Jesus.

Now, the 22nd verse of Hebrews 10 says,

> *Let us draw near with a true heart in full assurance of faith, having our hearts sprinkled from an evil conscience, and our bodies washed with pure water.*

This 'sprinkling' by the Blood of Jesus is what makes us have the boldness to enter into the Holiest Place, which we saw in verse 19:

> *Having therefore, brethren, boldness to enter into the holiest by the blood of Jesus.*

- Beloved, do you at any time feel that God is so far from you?

- Do you at any time struggle at the place of prayer to break through into God's presence?

- Do you at any time struggle to experience God's Awesome Presence?

The Blood of Jesus is your access!

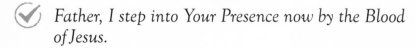

✓ *Father, I step into Your Presence now by the Blood of Jesus.*

✓ *I step into the Holy of Holies by the Blood of my Saviour Jesus Christ.*

✓ *I access Your Presence; I fellowship with You LORD; I experience You LORD; I encounter You LORD by the Blood of Jesus.*

What a Precious Blood!

What a valuable Blood:...

⚐ That gives us exemption from enemies' plagues and destructions;

⚐ That gives us escape from prisons where the enemy tries to keep us;

⚐ That gives us the tonic of Divine health and Divine life.

What a Blood that connects us to the blessings of God, and deletes the curses of life.

What a weapon of victory in battle over the

enemy!

What an instrument of cleansing and purification, that gives us access to the Presence of God!

Now you may say, 'But all this while, I have not seen all these results of the Blood you mentioned. I have not seen all the Blessings of His Bleeding by the power of the Blood as you've said here."

 Yes! What is not your revelation can never be your manifestation.

You can do many things from the standpoint of religion, but religion does not produce reality. It is revelation that produces reality.

The next time you apply the Blood – whether at the place of prayer, communion, or whatever, do it with this revelation, with full understanding, and full assurance, and you will see the manifestations of the power of the Blood.

Now beloved, isn't Calvary wonderful?

Isn't it wonderful to appreciate God for

Calvary?

Jesus carried our unrighteousness so we can take His righteousness.

He took our hurt so we can take His health.

He took our wretchedness so we can take His blessedness.

He took our 'cursefulness' so we can receive His 'curselessness.'

He took our place in death so we can take His place in life:

 HE DIED YOUNG SO WE CAN LIVE LONG. HE DIED THE DEATH WE SHOULD HAVE DIED SO WE CAN LIVE THE LIFE HE SHOULD HAVE LIVED.

He was despised so we can be esteemed. He was devalued so we can have value.

He was rejected so we can be accepted.

He suffered rejection so we can experience acceptance.

He took our grief and sorrow so we can take His joy and pleasure.

He took our pressures and troubles so we can have His peace and rest.

He took our place in hell so we can find our place in heaven.

He shed His Blood so we could have an exemption from the enemy's plagues and destructions, and escape from the enemy's captivity and imprisonment.

He shed His Blood to grant us full access to Divine health and Divine life.

He shed His Blood to connect us to the blessings of God and break whatever curses follow us.

His Precious Blood is our weapon of victory over the enemy!

His Blood is our instrument of cleansing and purification, and our key of access to the Presence of God!

Hallelujah!

Chapter Five

ACCESSING THE BLESSING OF HIS BLEEDING

The Blessing of His Bleeding

"Man that is in honour, and understandeth not, is like the beasts that perish.

Psalms 49:20

Accessing the Blessing of His Bleeding

> "You cannot apprehend what you don't comprehend... So, deepen your understanding..."

Everything you have read so far – from The Great Exchange to the Power of the Blood - are the Blessings of His Bleeding.

Now, how do you access these blessings?

» Receive His sacrificial death on the Cross for you.

Receive Jesus into your life as your Lord and Saviour.

John 1:12 says, *"For as many as received Him, He gave them the power to become the sons of God."*

Receive Him genuinely! Don't play church; be real. Don't just be a churchgoer; be real! Receive Him as your Saviour.

» Deepen your understanding of your benefits in redemption.

Deepen your understanding because your faith is anchored on your understanding.

The truth is, *you cannot apprehend what you don't comprehend. A journey you don't understand, you cannot undertake.* So, deepen your understanding.

Deuteronomy 29:29 says, "*The secret things belong unto the Lord our God: but those things which are revealed belong unto us and to our children for ever,...*"

 WHAT IS NOT YOUR REVELATION CAN NEVER BE YOUR POSSESSION. YOU POSSESS IT TO THE EXTENT IT HAS BEEN REVEALED.

Think about it: The Bible tells us that Jesus was despised so you can be esteemed, meanwhile you are moving up and down with a low self-esteem and inferiority mentality.

You are moving up and down struggling with the feelings of depression and rejection when all that has been taken care of by Calvary.

Psalms 49:20 says, "*Man that is in honour, and understandeth not, is like the beasts that perish.*"

Beloved, you must deepen your understanding of your benefits in redemption. There are some things you understand that make you behave in very rugged ways.

Some time ago, I said to my wife, "If I cannot

believe God for this, how would I be able to believe Him for that?"

Everything happens in phases. If I can't believe Him for minor things, how would I be able to believe Him for major matters?

When Smith Wigglesworth had kidney stones, he said, "I better die trusting God than live the rest of my life doubting Him, not knowing what to believe." (paraphrased). He depended on God for healing, and of course, he was healed.

I'm not saying you should do that if your faith is not at that level. But I'm using that to let you know you can deepen your understanding and grow your faith in God.

⟫ Appropriate your inheritance by faith.

A song by Deborah Enenche says, "*Even if you slay me or seem to delay me. I will never let go. Even if I'm lost at any cost. I will never let go...*"

That was what Job said.

Now, 'lost' does not imply 'lost in sin.' It means even if I cannot find my bearing; that is, I am trying to know my next step, but even if I don't know what next step to take, I won't let go.

That is what happens when you know what is yours. No matter what comes your way, you are ready to stand and appropriate your inheritance by faith.

Hebrews 6:12 says, *"That ye be not slothful, but followers of them who through faith and patience inherit the promises."*

 ## So, what do you do to appropriate the Blessing of His Bleeding?

→ *Receive His sacrificial death on Calvary.*

→ *Deepen your understanding by studying the Scriptures, reading books like this, and listening to deep undiluted messages.*

→ *Understand these things, take them in, force them to be real in your life, and walk in the reality of their manifestation.*

Beloved, please understand that light is reflective. Anywhere you see light, it shines. If the light of Scripture in this area is in you, it fences away darkness - the darkness of depression, affliction, and rejection.

I Pray for you

⊜ *That you will experience God like never before.*

⊜ *That the Blessing of His Bleeding will become real in your life.*

⊜ *And that the power of the Blood will be proven true in your life, in the Precious Name of Jesus Christ. Amen!*

Shalom!

THIS IS VERY IMPORTANT

Beloved, before you drop this book, I intend to address the most important issue, both in time and eternity. It's the matter of the soul. It's the matter of life. It's the matter of life after death.

A. Life is Terminal.

And as it is appointed unto men once to die, but after this the judgement: Hebrews 9:27

Then shall the dust return to the earth as it was: and the Spirit shall return to God who gave it. **Ecclesiastes 12:7**

B. Death is not the end of life.

Beyond death, life continues either in Heaven with God or in Hell with Satan.

And many of them that sleep in the dust of

the earth shall awake, some to everlasting life and some to shame and everlasting contempt. **Daniel 12:2**

The wicked shall be turned into hell and all the nations that forget God. **Psalms 9:17**

And there shall in no wise enter into it anything that defileth, neither whatsoever worketh abomination, nor maketh a lie: but they which are written in the lamb's book of life. **Revelation 21:27**

C. How you live on earth determines where you will end in eternity.

Let us hear the conclusion of the whole matter: Fear God and keep His Commandments: for this is the whole duty of man. For God shall bring every work into judgement, with every secret thing whether it is good or whether it is evil. **Ecclesiastes 12:13-14**

So then every one of us shall give account of himself to God. **Romans 14:12**

D. Who you live for on earth determines who you live with in eternity.

Neither is there salvation in any other: for there is none other name under Heaven given among men, whereby we must be saved. **Acts 4:12**

Jesus saith unto him, I am the way, the truth and the life: no man cometh to my father but by me. **John 14:6**

Beloved, in order not to end in a regrettable eternity in everlasting flames and torment, you must answer the following questions with all sincerity and accuracy:

1. Who are you living for? Who controls your life? Who directs your actions and lifestyle? Is it self, the world or Christ?

For to me to live is Christ, and to die is gain.
Philippians 1:21

2. What are the controlling desires of your life? What do you desire above every other thing in life? What drives you? Is it God, worldly pleasures or self?

One thing have I desired of the Lord, that will I seek after: that I may dwell in the house of the Lord all the days of my life, to behold the beauty of the Lord, and to inquire in His temple. **Psalm 27:4**

3. What is your public testimony:

Do you represent Christ to your world?

Are you living an exemplary Christian life to the world around you?

Who do they think you are?

> *And when he had found him, he brought him unto Antioch. And it came to pass that a whole year they assembled themselves with the church, and taught much people. And the Disciples were called Christians first in Antioch.* **Acts 11:26**

> *... be thou an example of the believers, in word, in conversation, in charity, in spirit, in faith, in purity.* **1 Timothy 4:12**

4. Does God know you as His own? Is He proud of you as His Child? Can you say that He is pleased with the way you are living your life?

> *Nevertheless, the foundation of God*

standeth sure: having this seal. The Lord knoweth them that are His. And, Let every one that nameth the name of Christ depart from iniquity. **2 Timothy 2:19**

And the Lord said unto Satan, Hast thou considered my servant Job, that there is none like him in the earth, a perfect and an upright man, one that feareth God, and eschewed evil? **Job 1:8.**

5. What are you looking forward in eternity? Are you sure that a pleasant welcome awaits you? If you had died before this time, where do you think you deserve to be, considering your actions, lifestyle and life priorities?

For I am now ready to be offered, and the time of my departure is at hand. I have fought a good fight, I have finished my course, I have kept the faith: Henceforth there is laid up for me a crown of righteousness, which the Lord, the righteous judge, shall give me at that day: and not to me only: but unto all them also that love his appearing. **2 Timothy 4:6-8**

Beloved, are your answers in the affirmative to

all of the above questions?

If not, it means you either need to surrender your life to the Lordship of Jesus Christ by accepting His sacrificial death on Calvary for you or you need to re-dedicate your life to Jesus Christ.

If so, pray this prayer with me:

Lord Jesus, I come before You today to surrender my life completely to you. I have lived a self-centred life that is far separated from God, I have had priorities that are not eternity-centred, I have always lived in rebellion, disobedience and sin up till now.

Lord, I am sorry for the way that I have lived and I ask for your forgiveness and mercy. Lord, please cleanse my sins by your blood and take your place of leadership and rulership in my life.

Fill my heart Lord with the right desires and priorities. Deliver me from the vanity and fantasies of this world.

Give me the grace to say no to sin and compromise. Give me the grace to live in righteousness and represent you well in my world.

Help me to escape the tragedy of eternity in hell. Help me Lord to make heaven at the end of my journey on earth.

Help me Lord to live both in consciousness of your presence and of eternity.

Continuously reveal to me everything that would make me unworthy of Heaven.

Thank you Lord for hearing and answering me in Jesus' Name I pray, Amen.

If you have prayed this payer, please do the following:

1. Send to us your name, phone number and contact address by email: info@dunamisgospel.org or by phone: +234 803 3200 320.

2. Become serious with God by identifying with a righteousness and eternity-conscious church.

3. Study your Bible daily to receive a word from God.

4. Speak to God daily in prayer and let Him know your feelings and challenges.

5. Disconnect from every wrong association. Don't

follow them to hell if they won't follow you to Heaven.

6. Speak to others about God. Share your testimony of transformed life. Be instrumental in assisting someone to escape hell.

7. Repent promptly. Do not sleep over unconfessed sins. Apply the blood over your soul for cleansing continuously. Live eternity ready.

The Lord bless you.

Contact Us

Beloved, we'd love you to share your testimonies with us at **info@dunamisgospel.org**

OR

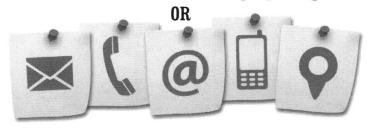

Write us a letter addressed to:

Dunamis International Gospel Centre
PMB 1677 Garki-Abuja

+234 803 3144 509; +234 807 2323 270; +234803200320

 www.dunamisgospel.org

 info@dunamisgospel.org

 drpaulenenche@dunamisgospel.org

 www.facebook/DrPastorPaulEnenche

 twitter.com/DrPaulEnenche

 www.youtube/DrPastorPaulEnenche

Worship with us @ the
GLORY DOME
Airport Road, Abuja, Nigeria

OR

Join our LIVE
services via DUNAMIS TV

Details on scanning for Dunamis TV:

1. Get a free-to-air decoder.
2. Press the MENU button
3. Enter installation (press OK)
4. Enter Pin (0000)
5. Manual Scan (press OK)
6. Scroll down to frequency menu (press the green button)
7. Enter frequency (12602) or 12600 for old receivers.
8. Symbol rate (26657) or 26630 for old receivers.
9. Polarization (vertical) if the horizontal does not change to vertical, then press the red button to change.
10. Finally, press OK for automatic scanning and wait.

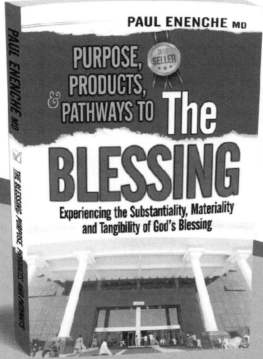

Step into the Next Level of Life!

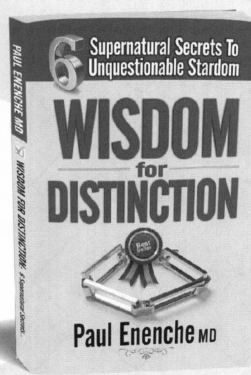

6 Supernatural Secrets To Unquestionable Stardom

WISDOM for DISTINCTION

Paul Enenche MD

> "The quality of your life is determined by the quality of"

This book presents six MAJOR principles that you should know and practice, if you must get to the place of stardom. These are the principles that have helped many rise up and stay up, and if you conscientiously go through this volume, you will never be found anymore at the bottom of life forever.

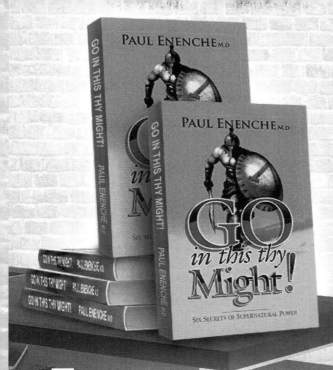

Are you hungry for the supernatural move of God?

Do you want God's Almightiness to be revealed in your life?

It's time to connect with supernatural might and be released to impact your generation! This book explores *six key secrets of might* that will help in no small way to facilitate your contact with the supernatural.

You Can Experience Supernatural Supply

that maintains its strength contrary to prevailing climatic and economic factors or forces; supply that has no respect for the economy or climate. That is the kind of supply that Isaac experienced during famine.

This book is a deep exposition on 21 Uncommon Keys to Financial Overflow. Learn the secrets and step out of every trace of scarcity in your life into the realm of continuous financial overflow, now and always.

PAUL ENENCHE M.D

21 UNCOMMON KEYS TO FINANCIAL OVERFLOW

PAUL ENENCHE MD

What was it that took
David, Joseph, Daniel, Nehemiah, Esther, etc.,
TO THE TOP?
You can experience their realm if you can decipher their secrets!

This book contains all you need to know to step into the place of value, trend-setting, and uncommon achievements in life.

AVOID **THE ERROR;**
LIVE THE SUCCESSFUL LIFE!

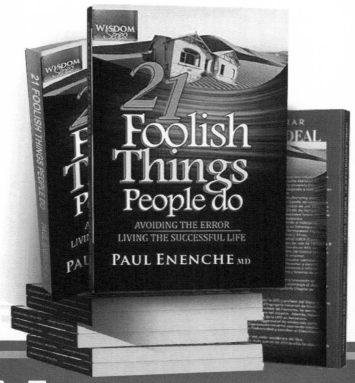

Many People are where they are today, and even go through several painful experiences in life, not because of how powerful the devil is, but because of the forces of ignorance and foolishness at work in their lives. This book exposes twenty-one foolish things people do - the very things at the base or foundation of every faulty life.

- **Carefully read through this book**
- **Study its deep truths**
- **Apply them in your everyday life**

Avoid the error, and live the successful life!

MAKE
SUPERNATURAL EXPLOITS
A WAY OF LIFE

- WISDOM PROLONGS LIFE
- WISDOM IS THE SECRET OF DISTINCTION
- WISDOM SPONSORS EXPLOITS OR MIGHTY WORKS
- WISDOM GIVES OUTSTANDING RESULTS
- WISDOM IS BETTER THAN WEAPONS OF WAR
- WISDOM UPROOTS MOUNTAINS

This book contains
**10 PRINCIPAL
SECRETS of
PRINCIPAL PEOPLE**
– the very operational secrets of wisdom.
Read it. Find out the pathways of wisdom,
walk in them, and experience Supernatural Exploits.

Index

Index

Index